S0-BBW-550

How to make
PLAY PLACES
and secret hidy holes

How to make PLAY

Doubleday & Company, Inc.   Garden City, New York

PLACES

and secret hidy holes

by Jane and John Lane

CHESTER PUBLIC LIBRARY
CHURCH STREET AT LAFAYETTE
WEST CHESTER, PA. 19380

101882

ISBN 0-385-13048-1 Trade
0-385-13056-2 Prebound
Library of Congress Catalog Card Number 78-14681
Copyright © 1979 by John and Jane Lane
All Rights Reserved
Printed in the United States of America
First Edition

to matthew

whose wish to bring home
every cardboard box he ever saw
inspired so many happy hours
of family activity

CONTENTS

A CASTLE

Imagine a pirate den. A secret cave. Two card tables can turn into a castle.

THE TURRET

Make the turret with a cardboard box. Remove top and bottom as shown in the drawing and have Mom or Dad cut the scallops for a more realistic look. Prop the box between the tables and drape sheets around. Hold sheets in place with pins or clip clothespins.

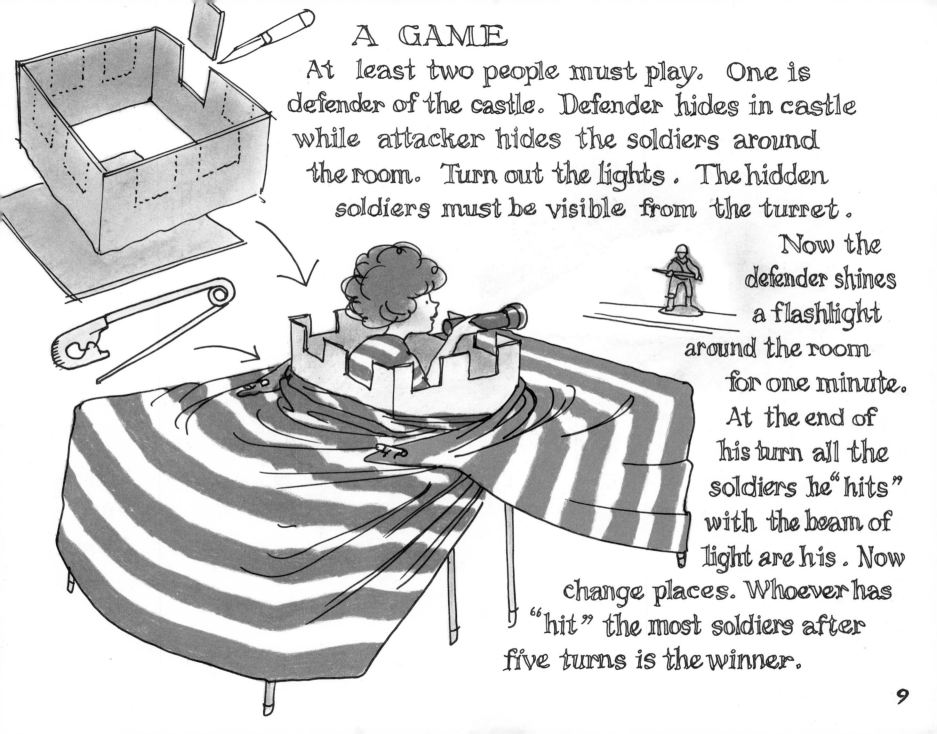

A GAME

At least two people must play. One is defender of the castle. Defender hides in castle while attacker hides the soldiers around the room. Turn out the lights. The hidden soldiers must be visible from the turret.

Now the defender shines a flashlight around the room for one minute. At the end of his turn all the soldiers he "hits" with the beam of light are his. Now change places. Whoever has "hit" the most soldiers after five turns is the winner.

9

PUPPET THEATER

back

front

door

stage

Make a puppet theater from a large packing box. The kind new appliances come in or the kind movers use to pack furniture.

If you can't find one ask a moving and storage company or appliance store if they would save one for you from their next delivery.

Then ask Mom or Dad to help cut the two openings.

LEMONADE STAND OR PLAY STORE

Use the same box as a lemonade stand or play store by placing a cardtable in front of "back" opening or building a go-through shelf on "stage" opening.

Instructions for the shelf are on the next page.

GO-THROUGH SHELF

90° 6" 6"

Ask an adult to cut
a piece of heavy card-
board the same width
as the "stage opening"
and 14 inches long.
Also ask them to cut
four, 6-inch, right angle
brackets. Center shelf
in opening and glue brackets
in place. Use tape to hold
brackets while glue dries.

INTERIOR SHELF

If you want
hidden storage
space add an
interior shelf.
Measure box from
front to back. Ask
to have a heavy
cardboard shelf cut
to that same length
and about five
inches wide. Glue
in place. Push two
straightened paper
clips through box at
each end of shelf
to hold in place
while the
glue dries.

POINTED ROOF

If you want your box to be as versatile as possible you'll have to point the roof. (The next four pages show why.) First, remove any shelves you added. Then ask an adult to make four flaps on the box by cutting all four corners down

bring sides together and tape

about two feet

cut off corners

about two feet. Bring flaps A and C together and tape. Ask someone to cut the corners off B and D and tape edges as shown.

A TUGBOAT

Add a box from the grocery with holes cut out for the windows. Coffee cans taped together make a good smokestack. If you want a steering wheel follow the instructions at right.

Lay big box over with "stage" opening down

(optional hardpart)
A STEERING WHEEL

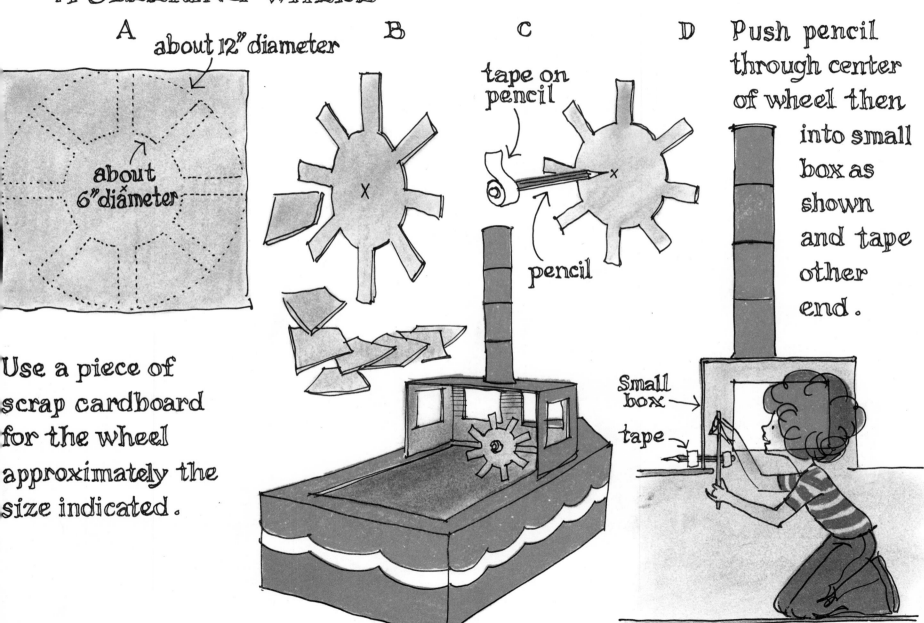

A — about 12" diameter

about 6" diameter

Use a piece of scrap cardboard for the wheel approximately the size indicated.

B

C — tape on pencil

pencil

D — Push pencil through center of wheel then into small box as shown and tape other end.

Small box →

tape →

A SUBMARINE

Add a grocery box to the top. Cut a hole in the top as shown. Make a simple pretend periscope out of a roll of paper or make the more complex one shown. It works like a real periscope.

Lay the big box over with the "stage" opening up.

(optional hardpart)
THE "REAL" PERISCOPE

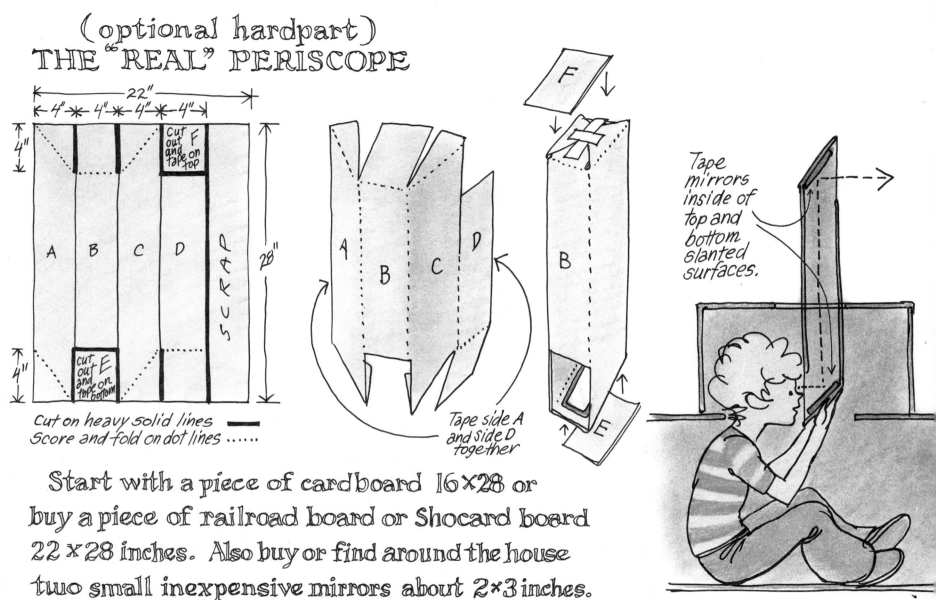

Cut on heavy solid lines ▬
Score and fold on dot lines ......

Tape side A and side D together

Tape mirrors inside of top and bottom slanted surfaces.

Start with a piece of cardboard 16×28 or
buy a piece of railroad board or Shocard board
22×28 inches. Also buy or find around the house
two small inexpensive mirrors about 2×3 inches.
We got ours in the dime store. Then have Mom
or Dad help you score, cut, fold and tape **per** instructions shown above.

TOY TRAIN

Little brothers and sisters should enjoy riding in this simple "toy train." Get a box from the grocery store. Punch two holes on each side and thread cord through. Tie. Decorate box. Tie several "cars" together.

COVERED WAGON

You'll need a box that will fit into a wagon. Ask an adult to cut one end out of the box and to cut three wire coat hangers as shown. Straighten the coat hangers out and jam ends down into edge of box. Loop over to other side and jam in that side too. Tape coat hangers in place so they can't spring out. Ask Mom for an old towel or sheet to use for the cover. Hold in place with tape.

ROCKET

Start with a large cardboard box. We found ours (the kind new dishwashers come in) on the sidewalk full of trash. We emptied it, shook it good, shook it again and brought it home. Our box had a wooden frame around the bottom. Not all boxes have this wooden frame, but if yours does, be sure to have it at the bottom of the rocket body. Otherwise, you'll have a top-heavy rocket on which you won't be able to make a point.

LEGS

Use scrap wood or old wooden mop or broom handles for the legs. We didn't have anything around the house so we bought four inexpensive mop handles at the hardware store. Tip box on side. Put household glue on box to measure about same length as half of leg. Tape leg in place with masking tape. Do other three legs. Let glue dry before standing upright.

POINT

Start by measuring across one of the box top flaps. (Ours were each 26 inches.) Next measure that same distance down each side of flap and make a mark. Go back to top edge and make a mark in center (in our case at 13 inches). Connect marks to form a triangle. Do all four flaps. Ask Mom or Dad to cut down two sides of the triangle. (Save pieces for fins.) Score the base line of triangle so point will angle in easily, and cut portholes. Bring points together and tape. Tape fins on legs.

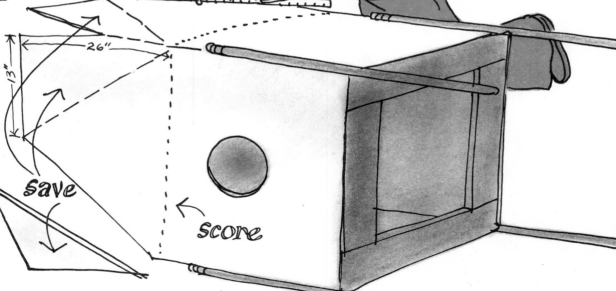

26"

13"

save

score

HELMET

Find a grocery store bag. Ask Mom or Dad to cut a hole at face height. Decorate with flag as shown. If you plan to encounter a "creature" in outer space, make a mask with antennae made of wire coat hangers. Tape on bag. Curl or put tape on ends so there are no sharp, dangerous points.

23

DUMPTRUCK

Make a dumptruck for your younger brothers and sisters. Let them fill and dump to their hearts' content and then take them for a ride. You'll need three boxes from the grocery store sized to fit into a wagon. Ask parents to cut ends out of two boxes; to cut end, side curves and windows out of "cab" box.

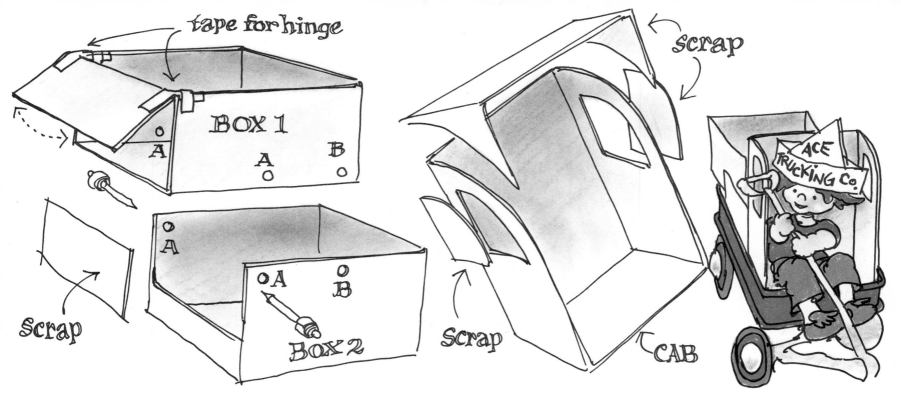

Next punch six holes: three on box 1 and three on box 2. On box 1 holes A go in center near bottom on two sides; hole B goes at rear on one side only. Put holes A on box 2 near front top on both sides; and hole B halfway back on one side only. Drop box 1 into box 2 so holes A and B line up. Get three pencils. Push one through each of the A holes and wrap tape around both ends so they won't come out. These two pencils act as hinges. The pencil that goes into hole B must be removed to allow truck to dump.

TEEPEE

To make a small teepee suitable for one medium-sized child or two tiny ones, you'll need four poles about four feet long. (We used the mop handles we bought for the rocket legs. Hope you saved yours, too.) If you want a larger teepee use larger poles and a larger base.

THE BASE

Start with a cardboard box about 10 X 13 X 11. Ask an adult to cut all four corners from the top to the bottom and to cut a small X in each of the four flaps as shown. Flatten box and jam end of pole into each of the X's. Gather poles together at top and tape securely.

THE COVER

Make in four sections. For three of the sections tape two double sheets of newspaper together. Tape newspapers in place at top and two bottom corners. Line scissors up with mop handles and cut out the triangular shape. Tape securely and go on to next section. On last section use only one sheet of newspaper so you have a doorway.

INDIAN TRACKING GAME

This game is set up much like a treasure hunt. One child sets it up; another does the "tracking." The person who is setting up must hide a series of clues written on pieces of paper. Clues lead from one to another. For example: Hide a clue in a sneaker in your closet. Write a clue something like: "In the closet

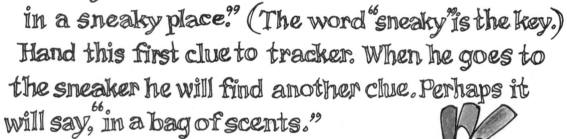

in a sneaky place." (The word "sneaky" is the key.) Hand this first clue to tracker. When he goes to the sneaker he will find another clue. Perhaps it will say, "in a bag of scents." This will lead him to a clue you have hidden where you store onions. (The word "scents" is the key this time.) Four clues should be enough for one game.

SECRET TALK

The secret language sounds so complicated that if someone doesn't know how it works, he won't have any idea what you're talking about. Add the sound "LF" after the vowels in each syllable of a word. Then repeat the vowel and finish the word. For example: "I am Chief Lone Wolf" would be said, "Ilfi alfam Chielfief Lolfone Wolfolf."

WINDPROOF SLED

Younger brothers and sisters will feel snug and warm while sled riding with a wind-proof sled. Make two holes in each side of box A. Run cord through holes. Fit box B into box A at a right angle. Tie boxes to sled.

ANIMAL HEAD

Decide whether you'll design your own animal head or use our design. Start with a piece of heavy card board one foot

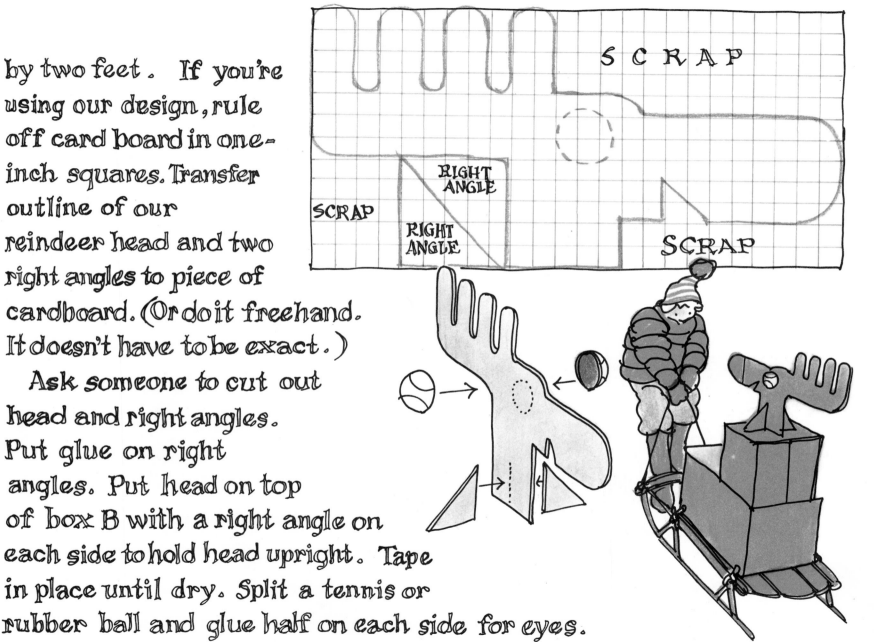

by two feet. If you're using our design, rule off cardboard in one-inch squares. Transfer outline of our reindeer head and two right angles to piece of cardboard. (Or do it freehand. It doesn't have to be exact.)

Ask someone to cut out head and right angles. Put glue on right angles. Put head on top of box B with a right angle on each side to hold head upright. Tape in place until dry. Split a tennis or rubber ball and glue half on each side for eyes.

LOFT

" How to " instructions for building a twin-sized loft bed are shown on the next eight pages.

As you'll see, possibilities for play places under, on top of and attached to the loft are many.

To keep costs as low as possible we used existing twin beds -- mattress and springs only on the loft ; an entire bed below.

An adult will have to do most of the work on this project.

MATERIALS

Pine: two 1 by 8's six feet 6½ inches long _____ Ⓔ

two 2 by 8's two feet 8 inches long _____ Ⓒ

twelve 2 by 4's two feet 8 inches long _____ Ⓑ

four 2 by 4's five feet long _____ Ⓐ

two 1 by 2's six feet 6½ inches long _____ Ⓘ

two 1 by 2's six feet long _____ Ⓕ

Hardwood: four 1 by 4 flooring three feet 2¾ inches long _____ Ⓜ

one or two 1 by 4's six feet 6½ inches long _____ Ⓛ

Pegboard : sheet measuring six feet 6½ inches by three feet 5 inches _____ Ⓙ

½" Plywood : sheet measuring six feet 3 inches by three feet 2¾ inches ___ Ⓝ

Glides : four _____ Ⓞ

Glue: all-purpose white

Screws: 56 five-inch No. 12 flatheads _____ Ⓓ

18 one-inch No. 8 roundheads _____ Ⓖ

24 two-inch No. 8 flatheads _____ Ⓗ

24 three-quarter inch No. 6 roundheads _____ Ⓚ

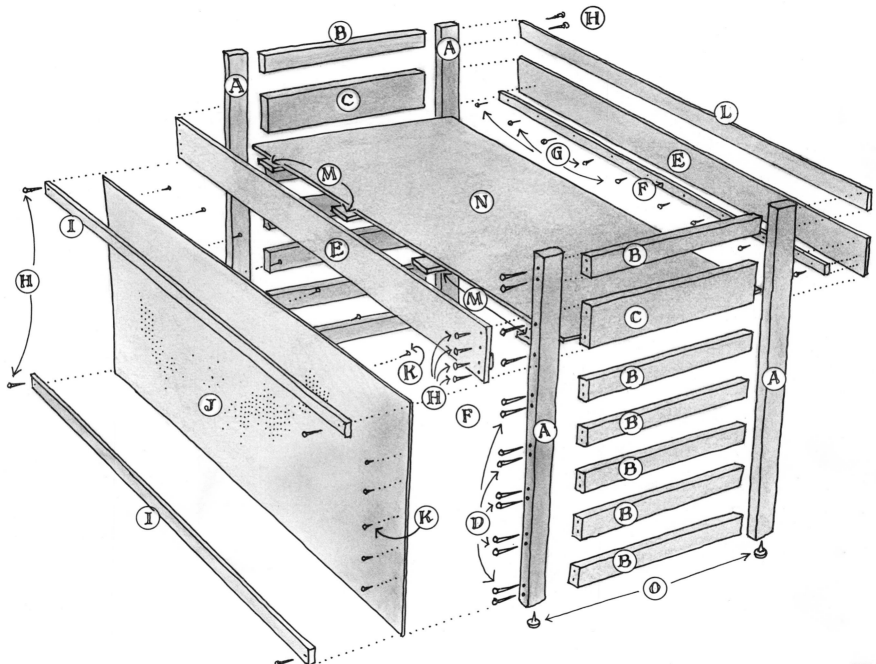

35

CONSTRUCTION
FIRST

Assemble two end pieces. Put vertical leg pieces Ⓐ on floor. Measure down each piece as shown. Drill holes through vertical pieces. Countersink. Line up horizontal pieces Ⓑ and Ⓒ and drill corresponding holes. Screw horizontal and vertical pieces together with № 12 Ⓓ screws. Fill and sand. Put glides Ⓞ on leg bottoms so loft can be easily moved.

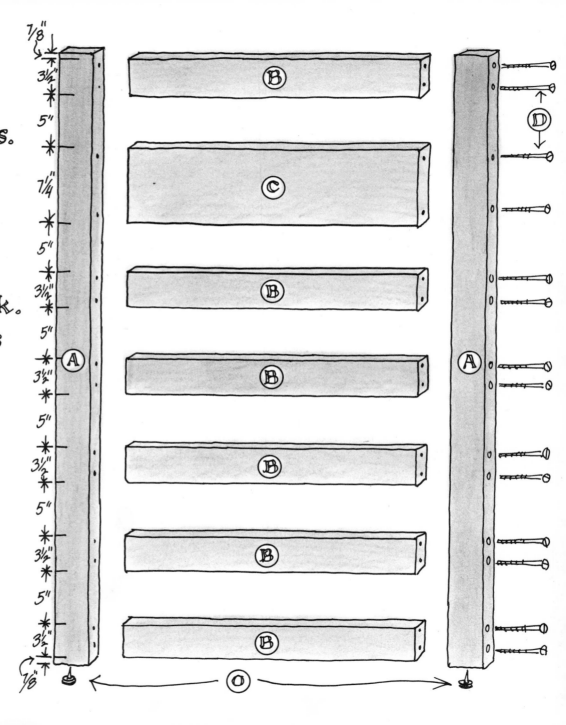

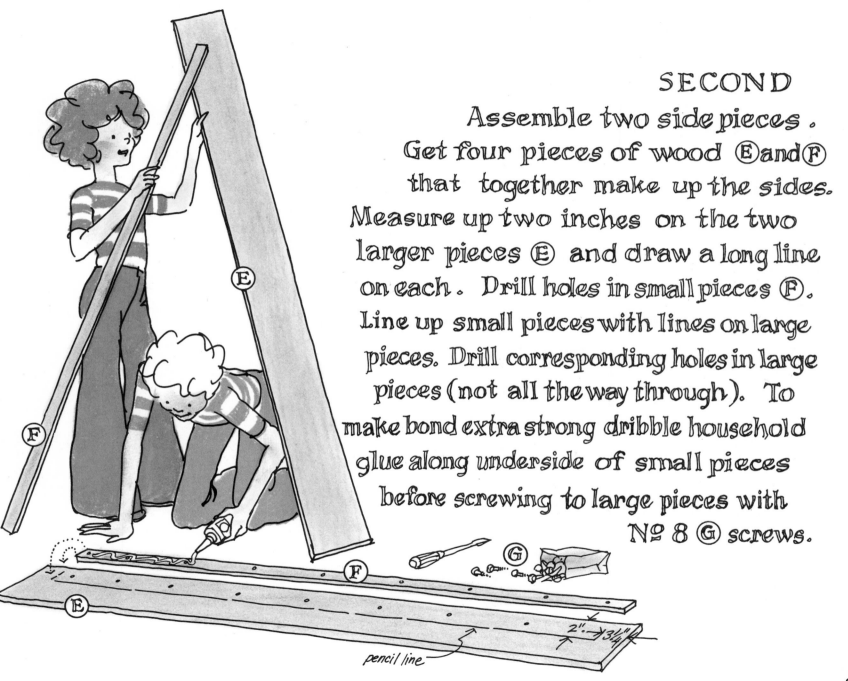

SECOND

Assemble two side pieces.
Get four pieces of wood Ⓔ and Ⓕ
that together make up the sides.
Measure up two inches on the two
larger pieces Ⓔ and draw a long line
on each. Drill holes in small pieces Ⓕ.
Line up small pieces with lines on large
pieces. Drill corresponding holes in large
pieces (not all the way through). To
make bond extra strong dribble household
glue along underside of small pieces
before screwing to large pieces with
No 8 Ⓖ screws.

pencil line

2"→ ‖3¼"

THIRD

Join sides to ends. Drill holes for screws. Countersink. Screw together with № 8 Ⓗ screws. Fill and sand.

FOURTH

Put braces on pegboard back. (This back is necessary for support.) Put two braces Ⓘ on floor. Put pegboard sheet Ⓙ on top.

Come in nine inches from each corner before drilling screwholes. Use №6 Ⓚ screws to screw braces to pegboard.

FIFTH
Attach back to sides. (Braces face out.) Use № 8  screws at each corner. Use № 6 Ⓚ screws along edges of pegboard.

LAST

Attach guard rail (or rails) L, drop in slats M and either springs or the piece of plywood N. (One or the other must be used so loft does not twist.) Use one guard rail if side of loft is against wall; use two if end is against wall. Mark drill holes at ends of rail. Drill. Countersink. Use Nº 8 H screws to screw rail to ends. (You'll need to buy four more screws if you need two rails.) Paint or stain and varnish loft.

PLAY PLACES

Put an existing twin or single bed at right angles to loft. Cover one or both mattresses with bright, washable vinyl. If one bed is not in permanent use, use it to set up on-going games and projects. Put bedding on when needed for a guest or have it made up permanently under vinyl. Wall or curtain open space below loft and make into a place to play house, a club house or theater.

If only loft bed is being used and all the space beneath it is open, use space for an existing desk or card table, a chair and light for reading. Or play games directly on floor.

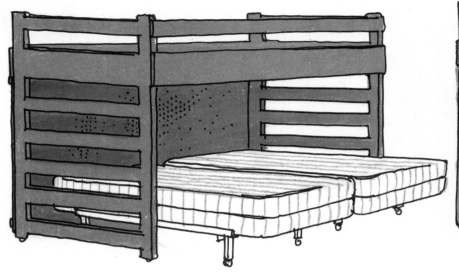

To make loft area into a play place, put plywood piece on slats of loft and use area for game playing or a train layout. Put double bed or two single beds at right angles to loft. Or put an adjustable steel bed frame in parallel to loft.

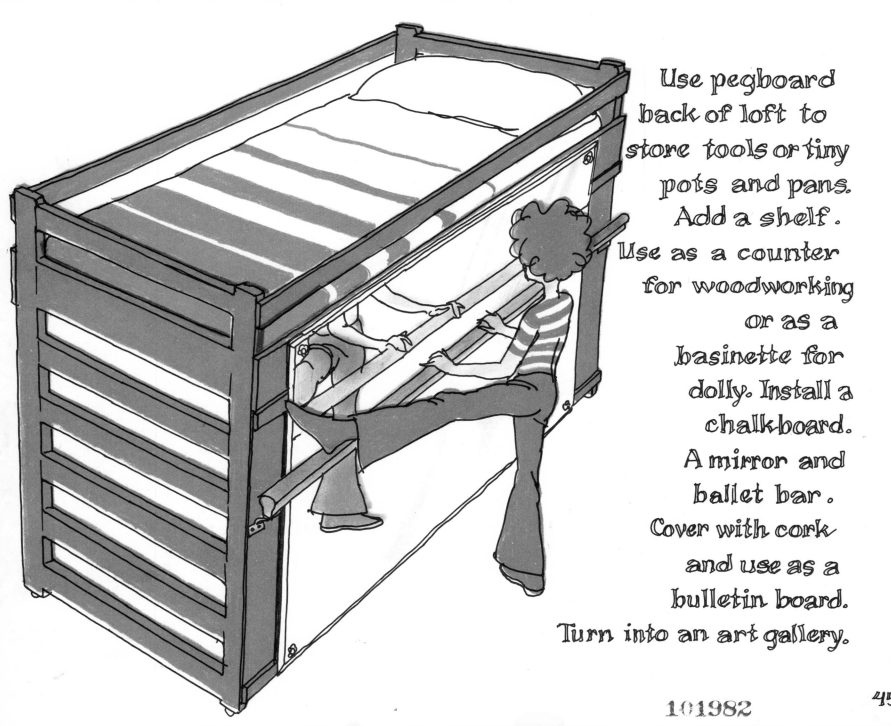

Use pegboard back of loft to store tools or tiny pots and pans. Add a shelf. Use as a counter for woodworking or as a basinette for dolly. Install a chalkboard. A mirror and ballet bar. Cover with cork and use as a bulletin board. Turn into an art gallery.

101982

JOHN and JANE LANE met at the Newspaper Enterprise Association in 1960 and were married four years later. They have a son, Matthew, and live in New York City.

JOHN LANE, artist and illustrator, is art director for Newspaper Enterprise Association and United Feature Syndicate. His illustrations are distributed to NEA's more than 750 daily newspaper subscribers in North America. He joined NEA as a staff artist, was an editorial cartoonist, and was creative art director for six years. He has covered presidential elections, the races at Daytona, and several major trials, providing on-the-spot sketches of personalities and events.

JANE LANE worked in the promotion department at NEA as a copywriter, as well as doing free-lance copywriting for advertising agencies in the Cleveland area. She has sold gags to cartoonists, edited books for NEA's publications division, and has shown her paintings throughout northeastern Ohio.

How to Make Play Places and Secret Hidy Holes marks John and Jane Lane's debut as a team professionally.